ISBN: 9798524308139

This book is dedicated to the work carried out by

Help the Persecuted.

htp.org

Millions of Christians around the world have lost their homes, their livelihoods, and their families to persecution. Many more are forced to evacuate and leave their entire lives behind. *Help The Persecuted* provides a wide variety of support to address their most urgent needs.

Royalties earned from this book will be donated to htp.org

Contents:

Introduction

The poetry contained within this book are some thoughts and prayers from a disciple of Jesus Christ. The word disciple is used in the New Testament to describe a follower of Jesus Christ. The literal translation of the word disciple is "apprentice". Being a lifelong apprentice of Jesus is what being a disciple is all about; to learn from the Master, to gain experience from spending time with Him, and to discover how to walk in His way.

There are fifty poems for you to browse and consider, a poem to celebrate each year of my apprenticeship with Jesus, so far. The poems are simple in structure and rhyme but are all written from the heart and it is my prayer that some of these poems will speak to you in a very meaningful and personal way.

I pray that some of these poems can be a help and encouragement in your daily walk with God and an inspiration for you to wake up in the morning with a new song in your heart.

I would welcome your feedback on any or all of the poems and which ones in particular had a special meaning to you by emailing me at terrypentland@gmail.com

> May our journey continue, and may the race be run,
> Until we are reunited with Jesus, God's beloved Son.

1. A glimpse of time

I am here on earth for a mere glimpse of time;
Everything I do here will face Your judgement divine.
You have watched over so many of us, through the ages;
It's a privilege to have my name, in the Book of Life's pages.

I think back over time, and all the love You gave
To Moses, Abraham, Daniel, David, all so brave.
You have included me among all the great;
To meet them all in heaven, I just can't wait.

A glimpse of time on this earth is all I am here for,
Three score and ten, maybe a few years less or more;
My time spent on earth from the day of my birth
Will determine my fate when I return to the dirt.

The choices I make, I will have to stand by
To face Judgement Day, from our Lord on high.
Every thought, word and deed will be judged;
Nothing I have said or done will be fudged.

Eternity waits; is it heaven or hell?
This is definitely the final bell.
Guilty as charged, and full of sin,
Only for Jesus, I would not get in.

Jesus stands up and says to me there
"Condemned to hell would be only fair,
But I paid a ransom for your soul;
No actions of yours could pay the toll.

"You took the opportunity while on earth
To believe in Me and gain a second birth.
You kept on believing as the days went by;
Heaven was always waiting when you die.

"Come to Me, unworthy but faithful son;
A righteous race you've run and won.
Spend all your time with My Father and Me;
Enjoy Our love and peace, for all eternity".

2. A new day

Thank You, Father, for a brand new day,
For the privilege of walking in Your way.
Thank You, Lord Jesus, for encouraging me;
Thank You, Holy Spirit, for letting me see.

A new day filled with Your love and grace,
A new day to get up and run the race,
The race of righteousness, to believe in You,
To continually thank You, for all that You do.

It's exciting to know You'll be with me all day;
It's an honour to sit with You, and be able to pray,
To share all my thoughts, hopes, desires and wishes,
To praise and thank You, for all Your heavenly riches.

A new day to see Your amazing creation,
To admire it all with such great elation,
To view Your mountains that are so high,
To behold Your universe, up there in the sky.

A new day to see Your hand on earth,
Plants and animals all giving new birth,
To see the range and scope of Your creation
Is to experience such a wonderful sensation.

A new day to speak of Your love,
A new day to be guided from above,
A new day to scatter Your seed,
A new day to help people in need.

A new day to pray for those who are lost,
A new day for us all to count the cost
Of the ransom You paid so we all could live,
Your death on the cross, our sins to forgive.

A new day for the sun to shine,
A new day that is both Yours and mine,
A new day to spend time with each other,
A new day with You, so much to discover.

3. Almighty God

Almighty God, full of such mercy and grace,
Your authority and love to keep me in place,
Your steadfastness, Your power and glory,
Your love and forgiveness, Your eternal story.

Your creation and beauty for all to admire,
Your grace and rich blessings to always desire,
Your wisdom and judgement that is so divine,
Your patience and understanding with that will of mine.

Thank You for the privilege of knowing You;
I will serve, follow and obey You in all that I do.
I will trust, believe and love You, with all my might;
My mind, body and soul will never give up the fight.

As I go about my day, please be there;
Let me feel Your presence, our love to share.
My desire is to please You in all that I do,
To seek Your kingdom, with the chosen few.

Almighty God, let me sing Your praise;
Let my old life be nothing but a mere haze.
To serve and obey You with all my heart;
Thank You so much for a brand new start.

Almighty God, so powerful and divine,
Your glory alone makes everything shine.
Oh Lord of Lords, and King of Kings,
I bow down to You, and my heart sings.

You loved me so much, You sent Your only Son
So that here on earth, Your will could be done.
I could now come to You, through Jesus our Lord,
To praise and worship You, sin put to the sword.

Thank You for giving us a chance to serve;
We know it's not something any of us deserve.
Your love and mercy shown to us all
Makes me feel, in my heart, ten feet tall.

Yours is the kingdom, power and glory,
For ever and ever, our eternal story.
We wait for a new city and a new earth
Filled with Your glory, a perfect new birth.

4. Being a disciple of Jesus

Being a disciple of Jesus is not a mere fad.
To be one of the chosen few makes me so glad,
To serve and obey the Master, each and every day,
To be willing to listen to what our Lord has to say.

I became a disciple when I was seventeen years old.
My French teacher, Don, he was ever so bold.
He preached about Jesus in a way I'd not heard before.
He made Jesus come alive, showed me the right door.

This door I knocked on, and Jesus let me in;
I asked Jesus to forgive me for all of my sin.
That night in bed I knew I made the right choice.
I committed my life to Jesus; He heard my voice.

I started my apprenticeship the very next day;
I took the very first steps to walk in His way.
Jesus started to teach me small things at a time.
He was in no hurry; we had a whole lifetime.

Being Jesus' disciple means turning up each day.
Being ready to listen, being prepared to pray.
Asking Jesus to teach me all that He can
So that one day in heaven, I will be a perfect man.

The apprenticeship is ongoing; there is no end.
So much has been broken, so much to mend.
Our relationship with God needs to be restored.
And that can only happen, through Jesus, our Lord.

Being a disciple of Jesus is a commitment, a lifelong task;
It's about listening to the Master and knowing what to ask.
Some days, Jesus, my Master, shows me so much;
Other days, it's quiet, not much happening as such.

One day this apprenticeship will come to an end;
One day there will be nothing left to mend.
Being a disciple of Jesus will be a thing of the past;
I will be perfect in the new heaven and earth, at last.

5. Blessed are the meek

Blessed are the meek for they shall inherit the earth
The reverse of what the world thinks, how perverse.
Meekness is not something that comes naturally;
Meekness is produced by the Holy Spirit, actually.

Being meek allows the Holy Spirit to control the mouth
When feeling angry and hard done by, wanting to shout.
To not want to say the things we sometimes feel like saying
Instead, for us to take a moment, and quietly start praying.

Those who are meek would simply never think to boast
Of any of their accomplishments; they will not raise a toast.
Instead, the meek give Almighty God the praise,
Knowing it was His power, knowing it was His ways.

Meekness implies there is a teachable spirit in us
Going quietly about our day, without making a fuss,
Giving up our future, our rights and even all our causes,
Submitting to our Heavenly Father, without any pauses.

The meek do not worry about what people say,
Unwilling to defend themselves in any way,;
No longer seeking sympathy or justification,
Leaving everything to God, with no hesitation.

To be meek does not mean giving way
Nor being quiet, never having your say;
Meek means standing up for what is right
Led by the Holy Spirit, never losing sight.

Being meek is what Jesus was all about,
Speaking gently, not having to shout.
Firm in His belief, humble in His way,
He teaches us how to be meek, every day.

So Lord Jesus, thank You for the Sermon on the Mount.
Thank You for all You said, making every word count.
It is the greatest teaching any of us will ever receive,
To be so blessed by You when we stop and believe.

6. Blessed are the poor in spirit

"Blessed are the poor in spirit", Jesus said.
To our selves, we must all be dead.
To be poor in spirit is to give up control,
To give over our mind, body, our very soul.

The kingdom of God will be our reward
"For being poor in spirit", said Jesus, our Lord.
So let me commit my complete self and my will.
Let my heart be joyful; let my heart be still.

Oh Jesus, what You taught so long ago
Is even more relevant now, I just know.
Poor in spirit means giving my total self:
That means feelings, rights, even wealth.

Oh Lord Jesus, let my self be removed;
Let me feed solely on Your spiritual food.
Let me be empty so You, Lord Jesus, can fill
Me with obedience and guidance, to do Your will.

I know there is a huge mountain to climb,
But if I trust in You, Lord Jesus, I will be fine.
But to climb the mountain with my own strength
Would be completely wrong, not what You meant.

The world wants me to believe in my self-reliance;
In the kingdom of God, this would be a show of defiance.
Self-confidence and self-expression are seen as success;
Your kingdom is the opposite, and You won't settle for less.

To be poor in spirit does not mean being weak
Or lacking in courage, or false humility to seek.
It's not about attempting to suppress my personality;
This would simply create a completely false reality.

To be poor in spirit is an absence of pride,
To be naked before God, wanting to hide,
Aware of how sinful and unclean I really am,
To always rely on God, never to rely on man.

7. Broken trust

Some people will just not learn;
From their sin they will not turn.
Their selfish will, the dominant force,
It keeps them on a wrong course.

I have a friend whose faith may have been lost;
She put her trust in her leader, at a great cost.
The leader had behaved in an inappropriate way,
The details of which she was reluctant to say.

The leader's actions affected a lot of lives,
Many brothers and sisters, husbands and wives.
Their trust betrayed in the most awful way,
How much damage to their faith, I couldn't say.

Sexual predators roam throughout the church;
They quote from the Bible, while ready to lurch.
They are sweetness and kindness, until they pounce.
Lives get shattered; they don't care an ounce.

Christian life is built mainly on trust;
Forming close relationships is a must.
To do anything to jeopardise that trust
Is a terrible thing than can happen to us.

To be a victim of such inappropriate behaviour
Can affect our relationship with Jesus our Saviour.
Don't allow bitterness or resentment get in the way;
Ask Jesus to help you get through this in His own way.

It will not be so easy regaining that trust,
But to be willing to give it a try, you must.
To give up on Jesus for someone else's sin
Is a price not worth paying; let Jesus back in.

Jesus loves you and wants you so much
He wants to encourage you, to rebuild that trust.
Jesus is so patient and will always wait for you.
Give Him a second chance, it's the least you can do.

8. By faith, not works

I had been on an evangelical mission to France
To share Jesus and offer folk a second chance.
I arrived home exhausted but felt quite a thrill
That I'd spent the whole summer doing God's will.

I then went to Galway to seek guidance and advice
From a special couple, Ben and Marty, always so nice.
People were there, being baptised in the spirit at will.
I too was so eager; I too wanted my fill.

A friend arrived in Galway the same time as me;
He had spent the summer backsliding, for all to see.
We both sought the outpouring of the Holy Ghost
Except I thought that I wanted it the most.

The laying-on of hands was performed on the two of us;
My friend began to speak in tongues without a fuss.
Meanwhile, I, who felt that I deserved it the most,
Just stood there silent, not filled with the Holy Ghost.

There was a rugby field located nearby;
I went there to plead and ask God, why?
I walked around the field trying to understand
Suddenly, the presence of God took me in hand.

The message came to me loud and clear:
"You feel you deserve this, I fear,
But it's not by works that you will be blessed;
It's by faith and grace. Now go home and rest".

This message was such a revelation, to see
God's blessings and gifts were not down to me.
I then left the rugby field with such delight;
My eyes had been opened and given new sight.

I returned to the house and asked them to pray.
They laid hands on me, and I felt right away
The Holy Spirit moving as I started to feel weak,
And then it all happened; in tongues I did speak.

Being filled with the Holy Spirit was a special event;
It was the most wonderful experience, heaven sent.
But perhaps best of all was the lesson I did learn:
That it is by faith and grace, and not what you earn.

9. Charismatic Renewal

In the nineteen-seventies, some fifty years ago,
The Lord Jesus came, and the Holy Spirit began to flow.
Throughout the land of Ireland where a lot of the folk
Got baptised in the Spirit, and in strange tongues they spoke.

Priests and nuns let go of their inhibition,
Raising hands to God, what an exhibition.
Giving and receiving a word from the Holy Ghost,
It transformed the Catholic religion the most.

Charismatic Renewal is what it was called;
This spiritual revival could not be stalled.
Young and old were coming to the Lord,
Confessing sins and putting evil to the sword.

Singing in tongues was a special gift;
All our spirits were given a real lift,
To praise God in a special tongue,
To give thanks to Jesus, His only Son.

The gifts of the Spirit were there to be seen.
Everyone joined in; we were all so keen,
To see the local people break away from sin
To open their hearts, and invite Jesus Christ in.

Miraculous healing was occurring in many a place;
It was quite the experience to see God's grace.
Prophecies were given with an authoritative voice;
Wanting to do God's will became our only choice.

However, the Charismatic Renewal did not last;
The end of it all seemed to happen quite fast.
Hunger for God stopped, and the people went away.
The singing had gone quiet; it was quite a sad day.

The Holy Spirit is something you can't control;
It has a massive influence on our spiritual soul.
The Lord gives and the Lord takes away;
The Charismatic Renewal had had its day.

The presence of God in all His might
Was an experience that set me right,
To worship and praise Him night and day,
To renew my commitment to His holy way.

To experience the gifts of the Spirit first-hand,
To see such worship throughout the land,
To share such fellowship and God's grace
Will strengthen me to run and finish the race.

10. Coronavirus

Coronavirus came, and we were unaware
Of the isolation that we all had to bear.
No one imagined we would come to a halt,
Locked up in our houses, no one's fault.

We take things for granted until they are not there:
Our family and friends, all the love that we share,
A simple kiss on the cheek or a warm embrace,
The joy of spending time together, face to face.

We amused ourselves with a subscription to Netflix,
Or using the internet, to join in with the social mix,
Working from home, Zoom became all the rage,
For others a lot of books to read, page after page.

Coronavirus started to spread its sickness;
Our bodies were showing little resistance.
Covid-19, a variant, had come to stay;
Isolation was the price we all had to pay.

Spare time was in great supply,
Time to reflect on when I die,
Am I ready to meet my Maker?
Or will Satan be the ultimate taker?

Now is the time to think about death
Before I take my very last breath.
Eternity seems such a long time;
The choices that I make are all mine.

Imagine spending eternity in isolation,
Spending every single day in desperation,
Living a life of regret, never to be let free,
What a horrible way to spend eternity.

How many times have I been taught
That my life on earth is worth nought?
Unless I repent and seek God's grace,
Someone else will take my place.

In heaven, where Almighty God does reign.
Where love is all, and there is no pain,
Where life is just and fair for everyone,
Thanks solely to the death of His only Son.

If we do not seek forgiveness here on earth,
Then we will never experience the second birth
That starts us on the road to eternal salvation,
Forgiveness and redemption, without hesitation.

We can freely receive from Jesus Christ,
Who surrendered His spirit and His might.
His blood was shed on the cross that day
So the Holy Spirit could be with us today.

Letting Jesus into our heart
Allows us all a brand new start.
Pleasing God is what it's all about,
Being in His presence, with no doubt.

This is a foretaste of heaven above,
Where God's glory shines, and all is love;
We have no idea of how good it will be
To spend time with God for all eternity.

To feel His love, warmth and grace,
There really is no other place,
But to enter, Jesus paid a price,
His earthly life, the ultimate sacrifice.

To make Jesus our Lord and Saviour,
We need to change our behaviour,
Confess our sins, accept His forgiveness,
Commit our lives to Him, our only business.

It's now no longer me in control;
The Holy Spirit is within my soul.
For everything I now do and say
Will always be to follow His way.

Because it's impossible on our own,
No matter how we strive and groan.
Pleasing God can only be done
By continuing to believe in His Son.

Then we can face Judgement Day
And only have one thing to say:
I stand before You, not in my name,
But in Jesus, who has borne the blame.

For on that cross Jesus has taken my guilt;
Despite my good works, nothing is built.
Only Jesus taking my sins on board
And me allowing Him, to be my Lord.

So as coronavirus has me in isolation
I give thanks to God, without hesitation;
To believe in His Son and have eternal life
Is a much better choice than eternal strife.

11. Creation

Father, You get such a bad press
And the world is in such a mess.
They say You do not exist, and yet
Everything around us, You did vet.

Your range of colours is truly amazing;
Your beautiful sunset leaves me gazing.
I get up early and see the sun rise,
To see Your creation with my own eyes.

There are the flowers for all to see,
Rivers, mountains, land and sea,
Forests, reefs and a sun to shine;
Surely all must come from the divine.

I often walk to enjoy Your space,
Praising You for Your amazing grace,
And our planet all so green and blue,
Something only You could do.

I travel the world and see different species;
It makes You come alive, no longer a thesis.
The colours and shapes, such beauty to behold
Lets my belief in You, Heavenly Father, take hold.

Everywhere I look, I see Your hand there
The range and complexity holds my stare,
Mountain ranges that are so vast and high
The stars in the universe, out there in the sky.

The diversity of Your creation for all to see
Is more than enough to convince me
There is an Almighty God who did all this,
Something only a blind person could miss.

12. Daddy, my Heavenly Father

Jesus told us to call you Daddy, when we pray;
It sounds too familiar. I find it quite hard to say
To a God so powerful and so almighty to men;
To call You Daddy means I feel like a child again.

To sit on Your knee and be an innocent child,
To be in Your presence, so meek and so mild,
To feel Your warmth as You give me a hug,
Oh Daddy, I feel so completely safe, so snug.

Daddy, there are so many things I need to know,
But being here with You, I want to take it slow.
Just being my dad for now is more than enough;
Let's leave it for another day, this other stuff.

When I was a child, both my parents died.
I found it very hard; I just wanted to hide.
But You, Daddy, You will always be here,
Never ever to leave me, nothing to fear.

Daddy, I feel so secure just sitting on Your lap;
No one can ever hurt me, not even a mishap.
You are with me forever; You will never go away.
Oh Daddy, it's not time for bed yet; please let me stay.

Oh Daddy, there is just so much to discover.
When I am not feeling well, You help me recover.
When I am troubled or upset with something small,
Daddy, You are always there, helping me with it all.

Daddy, it's so good just being with You
To see some of the things You can do,
To know You love me and all will be fine;
Oh Daddy, please be with me, all of the time.

Oh Daddy, let me take a running leap
Knowing You won't let me fall in a heap,
But catch me in Your arms to stay,
Keeping hold of me every single day.

Now Daddy, when I feel trouble coming my way
I will always look for You, Daddy, to help me stay
Peaceful and calm, as if sitting on Your knee,
Spending time together, Daddy, just You and me.

Daddy, I know that as the days go by, and I mature
That opportunities to sit on Your knee will be fewer,
But You will always be my Daddy, so smart and clever,
Always looking after me, and loving me forever.

13. Fasting

I love my food just a bit too much;
I find it hard to go without, as such.
It's important to fast now and again;
It helps me pray for the souls of men.

Fasting is a sacrifice not easy to make;
What if I fail? There is a lot at stake.
The devil will mock me for being so weak.
Forgiveness for my failure I will need to seek.

But fear of failure will not hold me back;
I am willing to fend off any evil attack.
My heart is willing, my flesh is weak,
Strength through the Holy Spirit I will seek.

I want to show Jesus I am willing to try
Just as He, in turn, was willing to die;
To go without food is the very least I can do
To show my commitment, with the chosen few.

While I fast, I want to spend time and pray
For souls who are lost and have gone astray.
That the ground could be prepared in the right way
So that the lost souls will listen to what I will say:

That Jesus wants you to accept
All the promises He made and kept,
To forgive you for all of your sin.
To repent and let our Saviour in.

To fast and pray, that the barriers be broken down,
To see you Lord Jesus, with Your sovereign crown;
To have men and women come before you and plead
To bow down and lay before you, their every need.

To see this happen would be a dream come true,
For lost souls to be found and to be born anew.
Fasting and praying would no longer be a chore,
Seeing so many lost souls love You, for ever more.

Join me in fasting now this very day
To see a heavenly revival come our way,
To raise our hands to God in wondrous praise,
To see the Holy Spirit work in mysterious ways.

Imagine a revival throughout the land,
A place where God's people will stand,
Of sinners who are willing to repent,
Of saints who fasted and did not relent.

14. Forgiveness

I wish I could get a good night's sleep!
Oh, that my dreams could be so deep.
No more turning on my pillow-case,
Trying to avoid what I cannot face.

Let my foolish pride not stay
So I can deal with it right away.
My mind is uneasy, my heart not right;
I don't want to have, yet another fight.

I've upset someone and caused offence;
There is simply no excuse, no defence.
I must apologise and hope they'll accept
My being unkind, ungrateful and so inept.

It's not that easy, swallowing my pride;
My conscience does not let me hide.
Confession is good for the soul, they say;
I am already feeling so much better today.

Forgive us our trespasses, we pray daily thus,
As we forgive others who trespass against us.
How often have I been forgiven by our Saviour.
Now let me forgive others, for their behaviour.

Forgiveness is such a loving act.
It cleans the soul; that's a fact.
It strengthens our relationship with each other,
Showing love to our sister and brother.

God forgives us through His Son;
Repent first, then your sin is done.
Don't hold back or even hesitate
To forgive others; it's never too late.

15. Growing old

As I get older my body starts to ache;
I'm getting slower, more pills to take.
It can be frustrating not going at speed,
To rely more on others for what I need.

I've stopped working, and it's time to relax.
I'm not getting any younger; let's face facts.
Time to reflect of a life in the past,
Knowing nothing I do or say will last.

It's time to look to the future, look ahead,
No longer to look back but forward instead,
Getting ready to meet Jesus, my Saviour,
To give an account of my behaviour.

I've served You, Lord Jesus, for most of my time,
Sought forgiveness and repented for any crime,
Been baptised to show my sins have been washed away,
Guided and lead by the Holy Spirit, day by day.

I know that I have not always done right;
It's been a struggle to fight the good fight.
I've disappointed You in more than one way;
On Your righteous path I did often stray.

But like the prodigal son, You welcomed me back.
You understood me; You cut me some slack.
Your patience and understanding is so divine,
And Your tolerance and forgiveness for this life of mine.

Lord Jesus, I feel the time is drawing near;
In spite of my sin, I have nothing to fear.
The day I shall meet You excites my heart;
The journey with You I can't wait to start.

The pains and illness, a thing of the past,
A new body given, a body that will last;
No more death, and no more crying or grief,
To always be in Your presence, what a relief.

16. Guardian angels

Guardian angels, just what are they?
They are always there when I pray.
Spiritual battles to be fought and won,
Soldiers of Jesus Christ, God's only Son.

One day, when I decided to go out for a walk
To a remote place, where Jesus and I could talk;
My foot hit a stone, on a path that was high.
I stumbled and began to fall; I thought I would die.

Miracles can happen to those who pray.
I'm not sure what exactly happened that day,
But I believe God saved me with His grace,
Placing a guardian angel in the right place.

Instead of falling over the side
Of the hill so steep that I might have died,
I felt myself being caught by a hand
That put me back on level land.

I realised what happened was divine intervention;
It certainly caught my immediate attention.
I praised God for His mercy and amazing love
In providing the guardian angel from above.

Now I know when I'm out and all alone
In remote places, with no mobile phone,
I have the confidence to be alone and free;
My guardian angel is there to protect me.

As I get deeper with God in prayer
My guardian angel will always be there,
Fighting the devil on my behalf,
Similar to using Your rod and staff.

There is a spiritual battle to be fought;
Your daily protection must always be sought.
Guardian angels have a major role to play
Ensuring that they keep Satan at bay.

17. Habitual sin

As disciples of Jesus, we can still all sin;
We can give in to temptation, let Satan win.
It's a constant struggle to walk a narrow road;
Battling with sin can mean carrying a heavy load.

Habitual sin can be the worst of all;
We try and repent each time we fall.
We promise we will never do it again.
Temptation is strong; we are weak men.

For many years I struggled with a habitual sin;
I battled and fought but never seemed to win.
Each time I called out to Jesus to forgive me,
Wanting to desperately stop; I felt so guilty.

This could not go on; I could sin no more.
I felt defeated just lying on the floor.
I would say sorry to Jesus every single day,
But the only solution was to change my way.

Self-discipline and control could only last for so long;
It could be a week or a month before doing wrong.
I was going to have to make one final last stand,
A gesture that had to be both meaningful and grand.

I do love my food; it always tastes so nice.
To give it up for a day would be a sacrifice.
So I made a promise I would go without food
For a whole twenty-four hours if I could.

A little later my habitual sin came back;
It was all-out war, Satan on the attack.
I had let my guard down; I had given in,
Disappointing Jesus with my habitual sin.

So without food I had to go;
The day had gone so very slow.
The sacrifice I was prepared to make;
My walk with God was at stake.

God saw my heart and my complete desire
To change my way, to put out the fire.
This commitment to go without food if I sin
Was the armour that allowed the Holy Spirit to win.

That habitual sin is a thing of the past;
It's stranglehold on me just did not last.
Thank you, Jesus, for being so understanding;
Your forgiveness and love is simply outstanding.

We all have to battle with a particular sin,
A battle of wills, to see who will give in.
No matter how hard it gets, try and see;
Jesus can do everything, for you and me.

18. Healing

Your gift of healing is so wonderful to behold,
To exercise faith, a faith that needs to be bold.
Sickness comes to us all, at one time or another;
It's hard to escape, whether sinner, sister or brother.

Some blood vessels had burst, a dressing applied to give relief
My leg was so tender, to touch would give me a load of grief;
I asked my spiritual leader, Ben, if he would lay hands on me
He said he was waiting for God's timing, to set me free.

A few days later, Ben said "I am ready to pray
For God's healing to come to you, this very day."
He laid hands on me and prayed with such strong faith
God miraculously healed me; I felt great.

A leg that was so tender and sore before
You could now hit with a fist; the pain was no more.
Crutches no longer needed, I threw them away;
God's miraculous healing would be the talk of the day.

We gave thanks to God for His amazing grace,
To experience His divine intervention, face to face;
To be given the gift of faith, so we can all believe
To be in His presence, see His healing power conceive.

Some thirty years later, the Lord blessed me once more.
I needed God's healing; I came knocking on the door.
My immune system started to be weak, instead of strong,
My energy non-existent. I needed to know what was wrong.

The consultant diagnosed a stage of leukaemia at this junction;
My body was not producing enough red blood cells to function.
Blood transfusions every month would be the cure for me;
A regular eight pints of blood would help restore my energy.

But my immune system was causing the blood to be rejected,
So they needed to refine the blood even more; I felt dejected.
The time would come, the blood, they could no longer refine
I knew I was in deep trouble, my standard of life much in decline.

I prayed to my Heavenly Father for His amazing grace;
I laid my impossible situation before Him, face to face:
"The doctors and nurses have done everything they can,
So only You, Lord Jesus, can heal this sick man."

God heard my prayer and answered without delay;
My need for blood transfusions went that very day.
The consultant had never seen this happen before!
It was a miracle; it made me thank Jesus all the more.

God is a living God, always wanting to reveal
His endless love for us, His willingness to heal.
The gift of faith from the Holy Spirit is all we need
To see the Lord's healing in action, a miracle indeed.

19. Heaven or hell

The human body is so complex yet robust;
How did we ever lose our thrust?
We no longer see You in life anymore;
Our selfishness has come to the fore.

Our evil actions cause You pain;
Our attempts to stop are all in vain.
No matter how good we become,
We need forgiveness from Your Son.

So many countries suffer strife;
This is not Your way of life.
It's to love one another, and peace for mankind;
With Your intervention, we can leave strife behind.

We see hunger and suffering for so many,
But so many rich people won't give even a penny.
Life is not fair, and we have made it so.
Hell is the place where most of us will go.

Hell as a destination is not set in stone;
The choice can be yours, and yours alone.
But you must make it without delay,
Or in hell eternally you will stay.

The choice of course is black or white;
The difference is like day and night.
A heaven where you never thirst,
Or hell, oh what could be worse?

I have lived my life and done no harm,
Helped other people, with kindness and charm,
Tried to do my best in every situation,
Helping the sick and poor, without hesitation.

Jesus says "No matter how good you are,
Man has fallen way too far.
In order for Me to let you in,
Man must be completely without sin."

Yet God knows this cannot be done,
So He decided to send His only Son,
To die on the cross and take our sin,
And that's our only entrance in.

"Many are called, but few are chosen," Jesus said.
It's too late to change your ways when you are dead.
So confess your sins and accept Jesus in your heart;
God's love and forgiveness will just be the start.

20. Heavenly Father

Heavenly Father, You have been so good to me.
You have enriched my life, Your blessings to see.
You have given me so much it's making me regret
That I have returned so little; I'm so much in Your debt.

You have always helped me when I needed it most,
Being comforted and renewed, through the Holy Ghost.
You heard all my prayers when I was in much despair;
You're my rock, Heavenly Father; You're always there.

Heavenly Father, You have shown me Your way,
Motivated and encouraged me, day by day.
You are so understanding and patient with me,
So generous and so revealing to let me see.

When I was sick, I felt Your healing touch,
When I was poor, You blessed me so much,
When sad, You comforted me with the Holy Ghost,
When I was lost, You helped me the most.

Heavenly Father, the traffic seems all one way:
You give me so much, thank You is all I can say.
No deeds or words of mine, will ever repay You for
Your mercy and grace when I knocked on Your door.

Heavenly Father, it's such a privilege and thrill
To walk in Your righteous way, to do Your will.
To spend time in Your presence, to worship You,
To seek Your guidance daily, in everything I do.

Heavenly Father, I wish I could give You more,
Never let You down, try and even the score.
Your love has no limit at all in it's measure;
I just have to accept Your abundant treasure.

21. Holy Spirit

Oh Holy Spirit, let my will be gone.
Holy Spirit, let You make me strong.
Don't let my efforts get in the way,
Dominate me for the whole of the day.

There are times when I want to take over,
Get drunk on selfishness, not to be sober,
Wanting to do things all in my own way,
Not allowing You room, having the last say.

Holy Spirit, You've been such a help to me,
Strengthening my faith, allowing me to see.
You encourage me so much throughout the day;
You show me how to walk in God's wonderful way.

So next time I am impatient and rebellious,
Please stop me in my tracks and tell us
That it's no longer my will that is in control,
But You, Holy Spirit, who lives in my soul.

When our Lord Jesus died and He went away,
He allowed You, Holy Spirit, to come and stay,
To help us overcome temptation and any sin,
To dwell in us, to let a whole new life begin.

You help me serve Jesus, my Redeemer and Saviour;
You are always there to help control my behaviour.
I want to give You room, to allow You a lot more space
So I can do God's will, and know I am in the right place.

Restore the relationship with God, my Father;
To be closer and not further apart, I would rather.
Mould my personality and my being from within;
Help me go about my daily life, without any sin.

So Holy Spirit, be with me day and night;
Help me always to fight the good fight.
Be with me daily as I run the race;
Help me finish it with love and grace.

22. Hunger

My hunger for You is a wonderful gift;
It excites my spirit, gives my heart a lift.
I want to feed on Your Word, night and day;
I never want this hunger for You to go away.

I am like a sponge wanting to soak up Your Word.
I can't seem to get enough; it all sounds absurd.
I can pray to You, Jesus, for hours on end;
Hunger is such a precious gift for You to send.

My appetite for You, Lord Jesus, consumes my day;
The hunger You have given me will never leave, I pray.
My eyes are wide open to learn more about You;
My ears want to hear about everything You do.

I've experienced this hunger from time to time;
It hasn't lasted; it's not really mine.
Hunger is a gift from You that allows us to grow
Without that appetite, my spiritual pace is slow.

I've spent years in the wilderness with no appetite,
My hunger dried up, my spiritual life a sad sight.
I've kept believing in You, I have kept the faith
But not had the hunger; I could do nothing but wait.

For the vast majority of my life
I have not had much of an appetite;
I have been lukewarm in my praise,
Not feeling Your presence most days.

It's been hard to concentrate and pray;
It's been really tough to walk in Your way.
To read the Bible and not have You reveal
Your divine Word, to make it so real.

I've waited so long for that hunger to return;
I've wanted to spend time with You, wanted to learn.
It's so much easier with a big appetite to feed,
To come before You, to submit my every need.

But now the hunger has returned at last;
The lukewarm approach is all in the past.
My heart is excited; my appetite is here.
How long will this hunger last, my only fear.

My heart skips a beat when I discover something new;
I get so excited when You reveal Your Word too.
This insatiable hunger, I so want it to last;
I want to follow, serve, trust, pray and fast.

It's so much easier when the hunger is there.
When it all dries up, it doesn't seem fair.
But life goes on, I will use what I've got;
I will always keep believing, hunger or not.

23. Imagine

Imagine there is a heaven, it's easy if you try,
A place to look forward to, whenever you die,
A place where there is neither sickness nor wealth,
A place where everyone is always in good health.

Imagine no hospitals are required;
Neither police nor judges are desired.
Doctors no longer have a job;
Psychiatrists are not listening to you sob.

Imagine having no aches and pain,
Not having to face a day of rain.
Money means nothing anymore,
Just love for one another ever more.

Imagine no more deeds of greed,
No more hungry mouths to feed,
Wars and battles will be no more,
No need for us to settle a score.

Imagine discrimination will be no more
Man's self-destruction is shown the door.
No bad mouthing or even an evil thought,
Forgetting all the bad ways we were taught.

For us there can be a whole new way
To make it possible for us to stay,
In heaven, a place without any strife
Because Jesus gave up His life.

He paid a ransom to get us here,
Took all our sins, His love so dear.
We must repent of our evil ways
And follow Him for the rest of our days.

Heaven could be yours and mine
By allowing the light of Jesus to shine.
Knowing this is just the start,
Loving God with all our heart.

Learning how to submit our will
Allowing our inner peace to be still,
Serving Him all night and day,
There really is no other way.

Peace and harmony will rule the place
As we live under God's amazing grace.
Sin and temptation will no longer exist,
And we no longer will have to resist.

This is what we need to do:
Ask for forgiveness and live anew,
Through Jesus Christ, whom God sent;
The one condition is to repent.

Then our sins will be washed away,
And we can have a permanent stay,
In heaven, where there is eternal life,
Everyone content and without strife.

But Judgement Day must come first
To determine those blessed or cursed.
Left or right, is it to be heaven or hell?
Only our Lord Jesus Christ can tell.

Many are called, few are chosen;
When we die, our lives are frozen.
It's too late to do any more,
Too late to enter the right door.

Jesus died to save us from sin;
That's the only door to let us in.
Good works, giving and being nice
Is not enough to enter Paradise.

Seek forgiveness and change your way;
It's a narrow path, so do not stray.
Jesus died for our sins, and by His grace
God's Judgement Day we can now face.

It's not by merit or efforts we are there
To face Jesus on the judgement chair.
It's His forgiveness and salvation alone
That will allow us to make heaven our home.

Heaven is no longer in imagination;
Heaven can be our final destination.
Heaven, a place full of love and grace,
Heaven with Jesus, the perfect place.

Oh what joy each day will bring,
Enough to make us want to sing
All praises and thanks to our Host,
God the Father, Son and Holy Ghost.

24. In the wilderness

Lord Jesus, please come and rescue me;
Being in the wilderness, it's hard to see.
I wander aimlessly both day and night;
I've lost my hunger, no spiritual appetite.

I was doing so well until my hunger dried up;
Being in an intense relationship, I'd had enough.
It was twenty-four-seven; I needed a break.
Now I realise this was an awful mistake.

My commitment to You needs to be every day;
Not just when I feel like it, not just when I say.
It's a lifelong journey with You, as Lord of my life,
Not giving up on You at the first sign of strife.

The wilderness is barren, and little will grow;
It's a lonely place that I have come to know,
A place where you can wander, with no end in sight,
A place that can't satisfy you, gives no delight.

In the wilderness, Lord Jesus, You seem so remote;
My throat is so dry, I don't even try to sing a note.
I want to praise and worship You as I have in the past,
But now I'm in the wilderness. How long will it last?

The hunger for You just seemed to disappear,
That feeling I had of You being so near.
All that was left was my faith and belief,
Just about strong enough, to relieve my grief.

Lord Jesus, please, I don't want to stay
In this barren place for another day.
Let my hunger and spiritual appetite return.
Let me trust and obey You; let me learn.

To be separated from You gives me no peace;
To be reunited with You will be such a release,
My eyes opened to see the Promised Land,
A land of milk and honey, a life so grand.

Thank You, Lord Jesus, for being patient with me;
Sometimes I wander off and just can't seem to see
That even in the wilderness, You will always be there,
Loving and supporting me, showing me You care.

25. Judgement Day

Life is unfair, we all agree.
It's so important for us to see,
That bad people won't get their way
When we all face Judgement Day.

God is just and will have His way;
We will all be able to have our say.
No thought or deed will we be able to hide,
Our beliefs and actions will determine which side.

Left or right, heaven or hell,
We all must hear the final bell.
Eternity is a very long time;
That's why Jesus paid such a fine.

There is nothing we can say or do,
Having lots of sins or even just a few.
It matters not how good we are;
Eternity in heaven will be a step too far.

Only Jesus Christ can let us in;
Only Jesus can forgive our sin.
Providing we ask Him, while still on earth,
We will come to heaven via a second birth.

Judgement Day we must all face,
To stand before Jesus in utter disgrace.
From our sins and evil that caused God grief
Only Jesus Himself can offer us relief.

It's too late to ask for forgiveness on Judgement Day;
Ignoring Jesus on earth is a heavy price to pay.
However, you're not dead yet;
Seek His love and forgiveness, and have no regret.

26. Just You and me

Oh Jesus, it's so easy when it's just You and me
To be in Your presence, to feel so completely free;
To be alone in silence, to be in a prayerful mood,
To have time on my hands for Your spiritual food.

I love the quiet stillness, Your perfect peace,
Wanting our time together to never, ever cease.
But reality kicks in, various people to meet,
So many things to do, brothers and sisters to greet.

Is it selfish wanting to be with You all alone?
Just You and me spending time together at home,
No distractions, no visitors or guests to stay,
Uninterrupted fellowship, for the whole day.

With no one to come knocking at my door,
I can study Your Word all the more,
Discover all about Your righteous way,
Seeking Your wisdom throughout the day.

I need to spend time with my sisters and brothers;
I need to share You, Lord Jesus, with others.
But every now and again, it's nice to get away;
Just You and me, Lord Jesus, time alone to pray.

27. Learning from Jesus

I want to learn all I can;
I want to be a wiser man,
To be able to see and understand
As only a disciple of Jesus can.

Open my heart and reveal to me
What ordinary people cannot see;
Let me realise Your amazing grace
And let me worship You, face to face.

Be my guide and show me the way;
Let me learn something every day:
The depth and vastness of Your love,
The power and glory of God above.

Let my ears be able to hear,
Everything you hold so dear,
So I can store it in my heart,
And never, ever let it depart.

Teach me, Lord Jesus, all I need to know;
Help me reap good fruit from all I sow;
Teach me to walk in Your righteous way;
Teach me commitment, every single day.

28. Losing our way

I have a friend who has gone astray;
He appears to have really lost his way.
He followed Jesus for such a long time;
Then I saw his behaviour go into decline.

We all face temptation and sometimes give in;
We will ask forgiveness for a particular sin,
But to keep repeating the sin, and show no remorse,
Well, that sets us all on a very different course.

When my friend keeps repeating the very same sin,
It gets harder and harder for Jesus to come in.
The longer it goes on, the more difficult it gets,
When not willing to repent, not having any regrets.

The best thing for me to do is to pray;
Ask Jesus to help him, in His own way.
Ask Jesus if there is anything I can do
To help him repent, and ask forgiveness of You.

This sin causes grief to other people as well;
How badly they are affected, it can be hard to tell.
So if my friend won't stop sinning and repent,
Then out of the church he must be sent.

God has given us all the freedom to choose;
Making the wrong choice means we lose.
If we harden our heart and do not change our way,
Then justice will be served on Judgement Day.

So if any of us are tempted to stray
We should allow the Holy Spirit to find a way,
To keep us on the road to salvation,
To join the chosen few in jubilation.

Jesus will wash all our sins away
If we repent and genuinely change our way.
The Holy Spirit will help us every day
So we will never again have to lose our way.

29. Money

Money is the root of all evil, they say,
Yet we need it to survive, day by day.
Money, merely of itself, is just a tool;
Money with greed, now that is cruel.

Money can be used to put a lot of things right,
Or money can be the cause of an awful fight.
Having lots of money can gain you respect,
But in God's eyes, it can have the opposite effect.

Jesus said to lay up all your treasures in heaven, not on earth;
You can't take any money with you, no matter what you're worth.
It's easier for a camel to pass through an eye of a needle, He said,
Than for a rich man to enter heaven when he's dead.

God can give to us and God can also take away;
Money can be a blessing used in the right way.
If God has chosen to richly bless us by His grace,
Then use the money wisely; spend it in the right place.

For we are mere stewards of the money we receive
To use it for God's will, before we take our leave;
We must be generous in spirit and always willing to give.
It's God's money; what a privileged way to live.

It's what is in our hearts that matters most;
We must give willingly when led by the Holy Ghost.
Don't let money lead to selfishness and greed;
Let it be used for the hungry mouths to feed.

Money can do as much good as it can do bad;
Money can make people happy as well as sad.
Use the money wisely, and your rewards will be great;
Treasures in heaven leave you in a much better state.

30. My conversion

I was just seventeen years old when we first met;
It was such a special day, one I will never forget:
A day when my life would change in so many ways,
A time to fondly look back on for the rest of my days.

I don't know what would have happened if we had not met;
It's fifty years later, and not a single regret.
In fact, I am filled with such a sense of gratitude and love
For the privilege of being reunited with God, my Father above.

You have helped me to make my life so complete;
To transform me from my old self was quite a feat.
I was so sad and angry, and my bitterness was rife.
You were so patient and loving; You saved my life.

I remember how I used to constantly swear and curse;
You took this in hand and made it instantly disperse.
I never cursed or swore again, from that very day;
It was a miracle to experience how You took it all away.

I realised how very wrong and sinful I had been;
I asked for Your forgiveness, for You to come in.
To come into my life and to take full control,
And with God, my Heavenly Father, to reunite my soul.

The excitement in my heart was quite a feeling;
I was bursting with joy, Your love so revealing.
Your peace overcame all that anger inside,
And all that hurt and bitterness; in You I could confide.

I got baptised in the sea to show God I had changed,
To show Him my commitment, my life rearranged.
Jesus, my Saviour, was now Lord of my life;
I would walk in His way, with or without strife.

Being baptised in the Holy Spirit was next in line:
To be filled with such love and peace, simply divine,
To receive God's gifts and to speak in a praising tongue;
It was an amazing thing the Holy Spirit had done.

I want to be Your disciple and to learn from You,
To serve and trust You in all that I do,
To worship and praise You with all my heart,
To be forever thankful for a brand new start.

Over the years that have passed, it's been a privilege to know
God's love, mercy and grace, to see our relationship grow,
And have Jesus, my Saviour and Redeemer, accept me as I am,
The Holy Spirit fill me with such peace and such calm.

31. My inner self

Heavenly Father, only You see me as I am;
I don't even see myself as much as You can.
To dig deep down way inside my inner self,
Seeing warts and all, I do need Your help.

Other people see what I want them to see,
Trying to be that person they want me to be.
But there is no hiding when it comes to You,
No false graces, no pretence in what I do.

Father, You see my heart exactly as it is,
Not dressed up, but shown without frills;
Stripped naked in Your presence, so exposed
Revealing what I want to hide, feeling indisposed.

There is no point lying, or being a cheat.
I can never win; it will always end in defeat.
The conscience You gave me is my guide;
I have to face up to things, not try to hide.

There is absolutely nothing hidden from You;
You know everything I think, and see what I do.
My inner thoughts that are both good and bad,
The deep bitterness inside that makes You sad.

Oh Heavenly Father, You know me so well,
Yet You still love me; I can always tell.
With my inner self exposed and laid quite bare,
You want to help me; I know You care.

Help me, Father, not to run away from me;
Make me stay, and see what You can see.
Expose me to show me how unworthy I am;
Forgive me, Heavenly Father, as only You can.

It's comforting to know You love me so much
After learning all about my inner self, as such.
The Holy Spirit will gently prod and nudge away
To reveal more of my inner self, a bit every day.

32. Poverty

A trip to the shops to get more than I need
Even though there is a hungry world to feed.
So much poverty and sickness to take in,
Not enough food, shelter or medicine.

We rich will have some price to pay
When it comes to Judgement Day,
Not helping that beggar in the rain,
Just walked right by him, yet again.

The hungry soul who knocked at your door
Asking for some food and a few pence more:
"Sorry, I have no change to spare".
Now I know life is just not fair.

It's easy to give money, harder to spend time
Making sure that that poor person is fine.
But treating the body and ignoring the soul
Is a heavy price to pay, an expensive toll.

Life is not fair; no one should go without.
Injustice and hunger exist, have no doubt.
But Jesus came to relieve all our pain;
The humble and the poor have most to gain.

Jesus has a very special place in His heart
For all who are poor and given a rough start.
He came to offer us a new life;
He came to ease our daily strife.

The poor will always be with us, Jesus said,
And their reward is in heaven when they are dead.
Suffering on earth is a price we all need to pay
To have treasure in heaven when we come to stay.

Meanwhile, let us help the poor in any way we can;
It's the least we can do, to assist our fellow man.
Give from our surplus; we don't have to go without.
Easing the poor's suffering is what it's all about.

33. Prayer

I cry in despair when You are not there.
I can no longer sense You in my prayer.
Yet by faith and trust in You alone,
I know that I will never, ever be alone.

It's just sometimes my mood is wrong,
My voice unable to sing a song,
My heart feels burdened and so sad.
I need You dearly to make me glad.

My mind wanders as I try to pray;
I don't even know what to say.
Yet You are always there with me
To dream a dream or a vision to see.

I seem to always burden You in prayer;
To unload my worries doesn't seem fair.
So many people are worse off than me;
My trivial problems make me feel guilty.

Yet deep down I really do know You care;
You say take everything to You in prayer.
You will always listen, no matter what.
Please believe me; doubt me not.

34. Presence of God

The presence of God is with us all day
And not just when we kneel to pray;
To be aware of His glory and might
Is quite an incentive to put things right.

How often do we need to say
I want to be good today?
Yet time and time again we fail,
All our efforts to no avail.

If we let the Holy Spirit prevail
Then we surely cannot fail.
Walking and talking with God all day;
Is there ever a better way?

His presence is a real privilege;
It keeps us on the narrow ridge.
To experience His complete attention
His awesome love for retention.

To spend every waking hour
Aware of His mighty power,
To intervene when we need
But only at His own speed.

To take time out of a busy day
To pray " Father, I just want to say,
I appreciate everything You do;
Thanks for being with me all day too".

I cannot see You yet know You're there,
Listening to every word of my daily prayer.
Faith and trust in You, Your love sublime;
To see You completely, it's just a matter of time.

35. Quiet and shy

I'm quite a shy person, not comfortable in a crowd
Mixing with people who always seem so loud.
I'm self-conscious and think people are staring at me;
When in a room full of people, I just want to flee.

I would simply hate to be in the limelight,
To be the focus of attention, to be in the line of sight.
I am so much happier just hiding away
In a quiet corner, not having to think of what to say.

Jesus, help me overcome my being so shy
Uneasy with lots of people; I don't know why.
But I know that if I submit this all to You,
It will no longer hinder me in what I do.

I am much more comfortable being one on one;
More than two or three people, it's not much fun.
As for being in a group of people, with me the stranger,
I just want to escape; I feel like I am in some danger.

The world wants people who are confident and strong:
The louder you are, it seems the more you belong.
But Jesus loves a person who is quiet and meek,
Who is happy to be alone, no attention to seek.

So next time you see a person so quiet and shy,
Make an effort to approach him; don't pass him by.
Talk about anything that will help break the ice
He will appreciate it; he will think you are nice.

God has given each one of us a unique personality.
Our interaction with each other is a different reality.
Whether being loud or very quiet, or boisterous or shy,
The Holy Spirit keeps on moulding us till the day we die.

So let's make an effort and be sensitive with each other,
Recognise the different personalities of your sister and brother,
Don't forget that the loud ones can sometimes feel so alone
While the quiet ones just want to spend their time at home.

Next time you are in church, have a good look around
And see so many different people that Jesus has found.
To have fellowship and share our lives, with each other
To be accepted for who you are, under God's loving cover.

So if you are quiet and shy all the time like me,
Let the Holy Spirit give you the boldness to be,
Part of God's church, with a vital role to play,
Interacting with each other, walking in God's way.

Say "Thank You for the personality You have given me";
Accept it wholeheartedly, and you will be free.
No longer self-conscious, the Holy Spirit in control.
Jesus loves every part of you, mind, body and soul.

36. Revival

Let Your Spirit flow throughout the land;
Let the people see Your Almighty hand.
Sinners would bow down in utter disgrace,
So they may experience Your amazing grace.

Brothers and sisters, come all, let us pray
That revival will happen, with no more delay.
The Holy Spirit will reside in the sinner's heart;
The people will be given a brand new start.

We'll see sinners on their knees, forgiveness received,
Giving thanks to You, Lord Jesus, no longer deceived.
Their eyes will be opened, Your Word to understand;
Your seed will be sown on rich soil, and not on sand.

The gifts of the Spirit will be received by faith;
We'll worship You together, in a heavenly state.
People will be healed from such bitterness and strife,
Marriages renewed between husband and wife.

We need You, Lord Jesus, more than ever before,
Praying sinners will come and knock at Your door.
Please create a hunger that only You can feed;
Let the people cry out to You for their every need.

How long must we wait while all is in decline?
Please hear our prayers and let Your light shine.
The people are lost; they know not what they do,
Don't realise what they are missing; they need You.

Let the Holy Spirit move in a powerful way;
Let repentance be the order of the day.
Instead of rebellion, we would all seek Your will
And walk in Your way, a new life to fulfil.

37. Salvation

Being saved's an ongoing process starting the first day
When I first commit my life to Jesus, to walk in His way.
It's not a single occasion, when I suddenly decide to repent
And ask forgiveness this one time; that's not what Jesus meant.

We have been separated from God since Adam and Eve
Sinned in the garden and were told to leave.
The only way back is through Jesus Christ, our Lord,
To spend eternity with God will be the ultimate reward.

Salvation is not just a once in a lifetime event;
It's a daily journey with Jesus, giving your consent
To serve and obey Him daily, with all your heart.
The day I decided to do this was merely the start.

Salvation is not just to believe, but to go on believing,
Not just to receive His love once, but to keep on receiving.
Salvation is a race that requires I cross the finish line;
That is when I will be saved, when salvation will be mine.

38. Self-reliance

Our stomachs full, money in the bank,
We don't always know who to thank;
When all seems right and life is fair,
It's good to sit back without a care.

But sooner or later, things can unfold;
Then we no longer feel so bold.
Our trust in our self-reliance is shaken,
Particularly when our employment is taken.

It's not long before our wealth will slip away
As we hope for things to get better the next day.
Self-assurance has started to take quite a hit;
Self-confidence is eroding, bit by bit.

I thought I was in control of life,
Regular holidays and little strife.
Now everything is tumbling down;
I'm facing life with a permanent frown.

What am I supposed to do now?
The situation is getting worse somehow.
My money is disappearing fast;
I'm not sure how long I can last.

Who can I turn to in despair?
Someone who is always there,
Someone to help me in my need,
Someone to forgive me for my greed.

I'm getting more desperate every day;
I am even on my knees to pray,
To a God I know little about.
Where can I turn to when in doubt?

Oh God, listen to my prayer!
Somehow I feel You are there.
I have been an arrogant man,
Believing in myself whenever I can.

Please forgive my sins and evil way,
For in Your arms I want to stay,
To feel the warmth of Your love
That can only come from You above.

Let me change my selfish ways
So I give thanks for all my days.
You heard my prayer in my greatest need;
You forgave me for my selfish greed.

I realise how loving You has been,
That Jesus died to forgive my sin.
No longer will I turn away,
Forever in Your arms to stay.

39. Shaky on Your road

Oh Jesus, You will help me in my need.
I know You will hear my every plea.
But sometimes it's so hard, yes indeed
And I start to get shaky on Your road.

Oh Jesus, I know what You say is true;
Everything You did, I would like to do.
But doubts appear, more than a few,
And I start to get shaky on Your road.

No one could ever do as much for me.
If I were blind, You would help me see.
But I find myself not able to break free,
And I start to get shaky on Your road.

Your message is so loving and so clear:
To be like children so we can draw near.
But it doesn't seem that simple, I fear,
And I start to get shaky on Your road.

Oh Jesus, You are so patient and so kind;
Help me get rid of my intellectual mind.
Belief, faith and trust is what I'll find,
So I won't start to get shaky on Your road.

40. Sharing Jesus with a friend

I want to share You, dear Lord Jesus, with a friend;
It's worth more than all the money I could spend.
I've talked about You while we both go on a walk,
But that's all it seems to be, just talk, talk, talk.

I want his eyes to be open, I want his ears to hear,
I want him to discover You with such a loud cheer.
A revelation from You, Lord Jesus, would not go awry.
Let him know You as I do; please don't pass him by.

My friend grew up attending church,
But unfortunately, it didn't amount to much.
He knew about You, Lord Jesus, in his head;
Oh, if only it had been in his heart instead.

Now hurdles and barriers get erected in his mind;
He listens to me sharing, but he is just being kind.
I want him to discover the full joy and peace;
I want salvation and redemption within his reach.

If he could only know Your boundless love,
Know the presence of God from above,
Know Your mercy, forgiveness and grace,
Please let him experience this, face to face.

Melt his heart with Your love divine;
Let Your beauty and creation shine.
Oh, touch his heart and conquer his mind
So Your forgiveness and love he can find.

Reveal to him Your amazing gift of life;
Overcome his ongoing spiritual strife.
Reveal to him the battle is won
By the death of Jesus, Your only Son.

Let him be born again and start anew,
Living the life of the privileged few.
Let him be received into Your arms, for all time
And know he belongs to the same family as mine.

41. Teach me to pray

Lord Jesus, I need You to teach me how to pray;
Teach me about all the right things to think and say.
Ten minutes here and there just doesn't seem fair;
It's hard to keep talking when You're physically not there.

I know You are with me in spirit all of the time;
Spending hours praying to You is a goal of mine.
To get deep in prayer and realise You are there,
Face to face, Lord Jesus, do I even dare?

What do I pray about for hours on end,
Apart from my deeds I need You to mend?
There is worshipping God, our heavenly Father,
And praying for lost souls; which would You rather?

Spending time praising God is top of my list.
Worshipping and singing in that heavenly mist
Could take up to a half-hour or more.
Oh, dear Lord, my knees will be sore.

Then next it's on to " Thy kingdom come",
Lord Jesus and His army, Your begotten Son.
"Thy will be done on earth as it is in heaven":
That's got to be worth a few minutes, say seven.

"Give us this day our daily bread", I ask;
That's now covered yet another task.
"Forgive us our trespasses, dear Lord", I plead,
"As we forgive others" who hurt us indeed.

I've realised now I've got prayer all wrong:
It's not about time or singing a song.
It's about my heart and mind being right
And fending off the devil with all my might.

It's about wanting to spend quality time
Pouring my heart out to that God of mine,
That God who graces me with His love,
Almighty God, my Heavenly Father above.

42. Temptation

Why do I seem to fight temptation every day?
Those evil desires just won't go away.
No matter how hard I try to resist,
It keeps hitting me like a closed fist.

Lord Jesus, You know how weak I am;
I want to please You as much as I can.
You say no temptation is greater than I can bear,
That no matter what, You will always be there.

Holy Spirit, please take full control;
Let me be the one to play the minor role.
Strengthen me with Your love and grace;
Put this temptation in its proper place.

Satan will not win this constant fight.
Jesus, strengthen me with Your might!
I will face temptation without any fear,
Knowing You, Lord Jesus, are always near.

Temptation will not have it's stranglehold;
My faith in You, Lord Jesus, will be bold.
As I walk down the narrow road,
My resistance to temptation will not fold.

My trust in You will come to the fore;
Satan will be shown the door.
Temptation is a battle to be won;
Victory has been claimed by Your Son.

Temptation comes in so many disguises;
Some to be expected, others surprises.
But no matter what temptation comes my way,
My faith in You, Lord Jesus, will be my stay.

43. The fall of Man

In the beginning everything was right:
Animals and plants, a brand new sight,
Heaven on earth, the perfect life,
Adam was even given a wife.

They could walk with God and have no shame
No pain, no death or even blame;
They wanted for nothing, all needs met
Enjoyed God's creation with no regret.

All the animals could procreate
The trees and fruits were in a perfect state,
There was full access to everything in the garden
Except to one tree; for disobeying, no pardon.

God said everything was free
Except for one very special tree;
The tree of knowledge of right and wrong
Could never be eaten from, all day long.

I don't understand it at all
Why did Man have to fall?
In the garden of Eden, everything was so nice
No bad thoughts, no evil device.

A place so perfect and divine,
A place for the sun to always shine,
To walk with God and be bare
And never have a single care.

Why would you let all that go?
Just so that you could know.
The tree of knowledge was your gain;
Little did you realise the coming pain.

God had provided for you in every way,
So why did you have to stray?
Right and wrong you had to seek;
Oh really, are we all that weak?

Satan has his subtle way,
Tempting us to often stray,
With Eve, it was the serpent's persuasion
That caused our downfall on this occasion.

Satan is a clever and subtle sod
Originally in heaven, he rebelled against God;
Now he was in the garden tempting Eve,
Using all his persuasion to deceive.

Eve listened and took the bait;
And the forbidden apple she ate.
Then she went to Adam to implore
Him to take the apple and have one bite more.

Satan can be a clever bloke
He felled them both with one stroke:
"Don't listen to God; be your own man.
Eat the fruit; you know you can.

God is afraid you will become a rival;
The tree of knowledge is, your own survival."
To no longer need God and be secure
That was Satan's ultimate lure.

Suddenly, they realised what they had done,
Their naked bodies exposed to the sun.
They tried to hide here and there,
Hoping God would not be aware.

God said "Adam, what have you done?"
All Adam wanted to do was run,
To hide his naked body and shame,
To not have to face God again.

Adam tried to blame Eve for his deed;
Eve blamed the serpent for her greed.
If either had confessed their sin,
What a different place we would be in.

Oh Adam and Eve, why did you give in?
Why did you both have to sin?
Life as God intended was no more;
Adam and Eve were shown the door.

Out of the garden they had to go,
Little remorse for them to show,
To till the land full of thorns and weeds
And mankind would inherit their evil seeds.

The price to pay was to send God away.
No longer was He able to stay,
For we were no longer pure in thought.
His forgiveness was never sought.

There was only one way back in.
In order to forgive our sin,
It needed Jesus to take the blame.
Born on earth, to the cross He came.

God sacrificed His Son, so we may
Die and be with Him in heaven one day,
A new heaven and a new earth to come
And to live with God Almighty and His Son.

44. The full armour of God

There is a spiritual battle being constantly waged;
Both heaven and earth are used as the stage.
The closer we get to God, the worse the fight;
We need to trust in Jesus with all of our might.

It's a battle where there can only be one winner,
A battle that will eventually eliminate every sinner.
If we all love Almighty God, then we must go to war;
Satan, the evil one, must be always shown the door.

God has provided armour, to fight the good fight;
Always put this armour on, and you will be alright.
If you don't put it on, things could start to get tough;
As the battle rages, you may have had quite enough.

Always use the belt of truth around your waist;
Make sure the breast of righteousness is in place.
Your feet should be ready with the gospel of peace;
Use the full armour of God, His protection to release.

Satan will fire his flaming arrows constantly at you;
Put on the shield of faith to extinguish them too.
Keep the helmet of salvation on you all of the time;
Use the sword of the Spirit, and everything will be fine.

45. The privilege of knowing You

I thank You for the privilege of knowing You,
Of serving and trusting You in all that I do,
The privilege of being able to receive Your love,
The privilege to pray to our Heavenly Father above.

I can't imagine what life without You would be like
To not experience Your peace, instead a life of strife,
To not thank You each morning for a brand new day,
To not be with You in spirit, to not follow in Your way.

Knowing You, the privilege is all mine;
Trusting You, my life will be just fine.
I'll go on believing in Your almighty power;
I will always follow You, every waking hour.

Knowing You has made my life so worthwhile;
Even through rough times, You have made me smile.
I rest in Your strength and security of Your love,
Allowing me to worship my Heavenly Father above.

Thank You for spending time with me,
For revealing hidden treasures I now see,
For the gifts of the Spirit I can now use,
Your love and grace never, ever to abuse.

Thank You for being so patient with me;
Thank You for paying the huge ransom fee,
And for forgiveness of my sin and being restored;
The price You paid none of us can afford.

It is such a privilege to know You,
To realise just what You had to do,
Facing the cross and being forsaken,
To offer me eternal life, my sins taken.

46. To forgive someone

What does it mean to forgive someone?
When you forgive someone, is it all done?
You have made the gesture in your head,
But it should have been in the heart instead.

To forgive someone is also to forget,
To let it all go, not have a single regret,
To have nothing but pure love and concern,
To never want to ask for anything, in return.

It's our pride that holds us all back.
It's our pride that Satan uses to attack,
Saying we were wronged, and it's not our fault.
It's this attitude that brings us to a halt.

We all need to let go of self to forgive,
To allow the Holy Spirit to teach us how to live,
To be meek and mild and humble too,
To be able to see others' points of view.

Lord Jesus, You have always forgiven me,
No matter how many times I fail to be,
An obedient servant, who serves his Master.
So often for me, it can all end in disaster.

Yet no matter how many times I tend to stray,
You keep forgiving me, keep showing me the way:
That true love means always putting others ahead.
Not accusing them but taking the blame instead.

Being led by the Holy Spirit to overcome strife,
Not to let bitterness fester, especially after a fight,
But to swallow my pride, say sorry without delay.
To be able to forgive someone, now that's God's way.

47. Trust

I'm in a pickle and can't see clear;
The problem won't go away, I fear.
I've prayed to God to hear my prayer,
Trusting Him for an answer, that's fair.

I still worry, my stomach does churn,
Yet God is allowing me to learn,
To trust in Him, and all will be right,
To let go of myself and not fight.

Let my prayer be yea or nay;
Never let my faith sway.
Don't let me hedge my bets;
It leads to too many regrets.

Seek ye first the kingdom of God, Jesus says
And His righteous ways,
"Then all these things will be added unto you".
Now I know what I must do.

Forgive me, Jesus, let the Holy Spirit in.
I confess my sins; let my new life begin.
In You I will trust for ever more
Now that You have opened the door.

Now I lay my worries on Your chest,
No longer hoping for the best.
From now on, faith is simply a must;
Jesus, You are all I need to trust.

Trust forms in us a very special tie;
It requires total honesty, not a lie.
It brings us all to the very same place:
Accepting Jesus, His love and grace.

48. What would Jesus do?

I find myself in an awkward spot;
Am I to do the right thing or not?
"Pay me cash and we'll call it ten."
Am I cheating the tax man again?

On the train, not paying the fare,
I could get away with it, but I care.
Telling a little white lie to avoid,
My conscience could be destroyed.

Man has a conscience over wrong and right;
It's a constant battle we all must fight.
I find the best solution for me to save face
Is to ask, what would Jesus do in my place?

Being honest in life is a constant fight;
It's easier to do wrong than it is to do right,
But my love for God is my measure,
To follow Jesus, my ultimate treasure.

The next time I face a conundrum,
I will ask what Jesus would have done.
I know the answer right from the start;
It's hidden away deep in my heart.

When I need to make a moral choice,
I will always listen to my inner voice.
I will ask myself, what would Jesus do?
The Holy Spirit will prompt me too.

There are times when it is hard to know
If it's right or wrong, or to go with the flow.
But stop and think, and ask yourself
What would Jesus do? It will really help.

49. When we die

What happens to us when we die?
We all want to know, but why?
Because if you make the wrong choice
No one will be around to hear your voice.

When we die, our bodies stop;
It's all over for the human clock.
Only our souls are here to stay
To live in heaven, I do pray.

When we die, our souls remain;
Eternal life is what we gain.
But it's too late to mend our way;
Our actions on earth will determine our stay.

All our life we had a chance to believe;
The forgiveness of Jesus is ours to receive.
Our life on earth is but a brief stay;
All too soon, we'll be on our way.

When we die, our spirit lives on
To face Judgement Day, right or wrong.
Without Jesus pleading our case
No amount of good will give us a place.

It's not a lottery where I might win
A ticket to heaven that will let me in.
There is only one entrance fee;
Jesus has paid it for you and me.

Without this, I will face death without our Lord,
Lying all alone in the morgue,
Realising what a mistake I've made
To let all hope of entering heaven fade.

If only I'd paid attention to my inner voice,
I'm sure I would have made the right choice,
Seeing Your beauty and creation everywhere I look;
But I rejected Your message within the Holy Book.

Now it's too late for me to have a change of mind;
Your salvation and redemption I can no longer find.
It was all on offer while I was still on earth;
I was too busy with other things of little worth.

If only I could warn my family of my huge mistake
So that they may realise and repent for their own sake,
And accept You, Jesus, as their Saviour and Lord.
To ignore You like I did, simply put, none can afford.

I'll spend eternity regretting my choice,
Being so lonely, no one hearing my voice;
Realising the love and peace that I've forsaken,
My place in heaven forever taken.

It's too late now for me, but not for all of you;
Places in heaven are only for a few.
Choose to believe in Jesus today and repent;
When you die, heaven is where you will be sent.

Heaven or hell, it's something we all must face;
Judgement Day is for the whole human race.
So make the right choice, before it's too late,
Because when you die, you have sealed your fate.

50. Worshipping and serving God

Heavenly Father, lead and guide us I pray;
Let no more excuses stand in the way.
Let every barrier be broken down
So we can see Your glorious crown.

Rule over us to Your delight;
Let none of us put up a fight.
Let us serve you night and day;
Let us obey You in every way.

What a privilege to love such an amazing God
Who guides and prods us with a gentle rod.
He is always so patient, so divine;
The good news is He is yours and mine.

Let us worship You, Father, with all our heart;
Let us spend time with You, never to be apart.
Let us believe and love You, with all our might;
Let us run the race, and fight the good fight.

To serve You is nothing but a pleasure;
To obey You is storing up treasure.
To trust You daily is faith in action,
Following You blindly, without a reaction.

Heavenly Father, You are so powerful and divine,
Your love and forgiveness, Your glory that shines,
Your steadfastness and faithfulness always there,
Your amazing grace, such a wonderful gift to share.

Worshipping You is a privilege I am truly grateful for;
Receiving Your grace makes me love You all the more.
Serving You with all my heart and all my strength
Is everything I want to do, and I will go to any length.

Printed in Great Britain
by Amazon

64973000R00061